# The Tales of
# NASRETTİN HOCA

SILK ROAD
PUBLICATIONS

# FOREWORD

Nasrettin Hoca (Hoca meaning teacher or preacher; pronounced Ho-dja) has been the dominant figure of humor and satire in Turkey since the 13th century. His anecdotes and tales represent the solutions that the collective imagination of the Turks has brought to bear upon life's diverse and complex problems. As such, they defy being indexed or categorized. Any attempt to do so is bound to serve an editor's subjective preferences rather than reflect scholarly criteria or help the readers.

In various collections, Hoca stories are grouped chronologically -childhood, youth, old age, etc. Some compilations are organized according to themes like credos or mores of social life. Still others follow such categories as Hoca's relations - with his wife, his son or his dokey.

We have avoided categories. Yet in view of the fact that the morals or punch-lines of some Hoca stories have evolved into proverbs, idioms or openers, we have grouped the anecdotes of this type in Part I of this book.

Although some scholars believe that Nasrettin Hoca lived dur-ing the 13th century, some advance the theory that he lived in the 14th century (which explains his many encounters with Ta-murlane who died in 1405).

# EAT, MY FUR-COAT, EAT

Hoca is invited to a banquet. He goes there in his everyday clothes: No one pays attention to him. He is taken aback. He rushes home, puts his luxurious fur-coat on, and returns to the banquet. This time, he is met at the entrance and led up to the dais where he is given the choicest seat. When soup is served, Hoca dunks the lapel in the bowl saying "Please have some! Eat, my fur-coat, eat! Eat, my fur-coat, eat!"

In amazement, some people ask him why he is doing this. Hoca answers: "The fur-coat gets the best treat; so, the fur-coat should eat."

# PEBBLE COUNT

People often ask Hoca what day of the month of fasting it is. To keep track of the days, he throws a pebble into his pot every day. When somebody asks him, he counts the pebbles and tells him what day it is. A joker finds out about this and throws a lot of pebbles into the pot when Hoca isn't around.

The following day someone asks Hoca: "What day is this?" Hoca goes home to count the pebbles - and what should he see? There are 150 pebbles. He mumbles to himself: "Our month of fasting has never been this long. I better reduce the number." He says to the man "This is the 45th day of the month." The man is perplexed: "Hoca, how can there be 45 days in a month?" "Good thing," Hoca says, "I reduced the number. If we were to go by the pebble count, this would have been the 150th day of the month."

# GREENHORN NIGHTINGALE

Hoca goes into an orchard and climbs an apricot tree. While he is busy gobbling the apricots, the owner rushes over: "What are you doing up there?"

"I'm a nightingale," Hoca explains. "I'm warbling."

The man challenges him: "All right, lets's hear you warble." Trying to sing like a nightingale, Hoca makes awful sounds.

The owner of the orchard is aghast: "What sort of nightingale singing is this?'

Hoca says to him: "Greenhorn nightingale sings this way."

# THE QUILT IS GONE, THE FIGHT IS DONE

One night Hoca hears a commotion outside. He is curious. He jumps out of the bed ignoring his wife's cautionary words - "What does it matter to you?" Wrapped in his quilt, he goes out into the cold night. Two men are fighting. Before Hoca can say "Stop fighting, will you?" one of the men snatches the quilt and runs away. The other man also disappears. When Hoca goes back into the house trembling, his wife asks him: "What was the fighting about?"

"About our quilt," says Hoca. "The quilt is gone, the fight is done."

# CAMEL'S HEAD

Nasrettin Hoca's wife spins fiber into yarn - and he makes balls of wool which he sells to the dealers at the marketplace. The dealers swindle Hoca and pay him much less than the value of Hoca's and his wife's work. One day Hoca finds a camel's head on the road. He takes it home, threads the yarn around the head, and makes a huge ball of wool. He takes it to the marketplace where, as usual, the dealer offers a price well below its actual value. Hoca accepts the low price since the bulk of the ball of wool is the camel's head, but the dealer becomes suspicious:

"Hoca, is it possible there is something else in this?" "Sure," says Hoca, "A camel's head..."

When the dealer runs into Hoca next day, he chides him: "A camel's head came out of the ball of wool. Aren't you ashamed of cheating?" Hoca retorts: "I told you the truth. Remember, I said it's a camel's head..."

# IF THE MOUNTAIN DOESN'T COME TO THE MINSTREL

Hoca keeps boasting that he is a saint. Someone challenges him to work a miracle. Hoca asks: "What sort of miracle?" The man replies: "Make the mountain over there come to you."

Hoca calls out three times: "Come to me, mighty mountain, cooome!" Then he starts to walk toward the mountain. The man says: "Hoca, the mountain doesn't even budge an inch."

As he heads for the mountain, Hoca replies: "I am a humble person. If the mountain doesn't come to the minstrel, the minstrel goes to the mountain."

# KNOW-IT-ALL TURBAN

An illiterate man receives a letter and asks Hoca to read it for him. Hoca does his best to depicher, but fails to make it out: The letter is probably in Arabic or Persian. "I can't read it," he confesses. "Have someone else read it."

The man gets angry: "You are supposed to be a learned man, a teacher. You ought to be ashamed of the turban you're wearing."

Hoca takes his turban off, puts it on the man's head, and says: "If you think the turban knows it all, see if you can read the letter!"

# KEEP YOUR FEET WARM

Somebody asks Hoca if he has expertise in the medical profession. When Hoca answers he does, he is asked what he knows - and he obliges:
"Keep your feet warm and your head cool;
"Keep yourself busy and don't brood as a rule."

# LET'S DIE A LITTLE TOO

One year, the month of fasting is right in the middle of scorching summer. A wealthy man invites Hoca to break fast at his house. Normally soup is served first, but because of the heat they serve iced compote. The host, who enjoys practical jokes, has placed a tiny tea-spoon before each guest - and he has a big scoop in his hand. Every time he scoops up the iced compote, he intones: "Oooh, it's so good I could die."
Hoca takes one look, 'then another, and finally he cannot restrain himself: "Sir," he says, "how about passing the scoop around so that we too can die a little."

# DID THE BURGLAR DO NO WRONG?

Hoca's donkey gets stolen. His neighbors come over. One of them asks: "Hoca, why did you neglect to replace this rotting door with a solid one?" Another neighbor observes: "Look, you forgot to lock the door." Yet another scolds him: 'The burglar goes into the barn and takes the donkey out of there - and you sleep right through? Hoca, how could you sleep like that and never wake up?"
In short, everybody finds fault with Hoca who can no longer stand it. "Look here, neighbors," he says. "Be fair, will you? Am I to be blamed for the whole thing? Did the burglar do no wrong?"

# LEGS OF GOOSE

Nasrettin Hoca roasts a goose to take it to Tamurlane. On the way, he gets hungry, breaks off a leg and eats it. At the dinner-table, Tamurlane notices that the goose is missing a leg and inquires: "Hoca, what's become of one of the legs of this goose?"

Hoca looks out the window and catches sight of the geese by the fountain: All the geese have pulled one leg in and they are standing on one foot. No sooner than he sees the geese he shows them to Tamurlane: "There," he says, "in our country, all the geese have a single leg." Tamurlane is incredulous. He calls someone in his retinue over and whispers his orders into the man's ear. In a short while, drums, clarinets, tambourines and cymbals are heard outside -and the geese, frightened by the uproar, flee for their lives.

"See, Hoca," says Tamurlane, "that's not the way with the legs of geese. All of these have two legs."

Hoca retorts: "If all that racket had been made for you, you would have had four legs."

# SPRINKLING FLOUR ON THE CLOTHESLINE

A neighbor comes to Hoca and asks if he could borrow a clothesline. Hoca goes inside and returns a few minutes later.

"I'm sorry," he says. "They've sprinkled flour on the clothesline."

"Come on, Hoca," says the neighbor. "How could anyone sprinkle flour on a clothesline?"

Hoca replies: "When one doesn't want to lend it."

## I'VE GOT THE RECIPE

Hoca buys a fine slice of liver at the butcher. On his way home, he runs into a friend who tells him how to make liver stew. Hoca says: "I'm bound to forget it. Please write the recipe on a piece of paper." And his friend writes it down.

Hoca is walking home, liver in one hand, the recipe in the other, when suddenly a kite swoops down and snatches the liver away. Hoca gives the kite a few minutes' chase. It's no use. When he realizes that he cannot catch the bird, he holds the recipe up and shouts:

"It'll do you no good. I've got the recipe."

## BETTER IN THE BELLY THAN IN THE HEAD

Hoca's wife prepares a heavenly dessert for the holidays. It is the highlight of the dinner. They eat it with great joy. They decide to keep the rest for lunch next day. But Hoca cannot fall asleep. Finally he pokes and wakens his wife.

"Honey," he says, "run along and bring the dessert."

His wife gets the dessert. They sit down and eat it all.

"That's it," says Hoca, "Now let's go back to bed and get some sleep. It's better to have the dessert in my belly than on my mind.

## AS LONG AS YOU'RE NOT INSIDE

They ask Hoca: "In a funeral procession, should one walk in front of the casket, behind it, on the right hand side or on the left hand side?" Hoca replies: "You can be on any side as long as you're not inside."

## NEVER FRIGHTEN MULES CARRYING CROCKERY

While taking a walk at the graveyard, Hoca trips and falls into a pit. He lies there for a few minutes and thinks to himself: "I wonder if what they say is true: Will the angels come to interrogate me?" In a short while, he hears from afar the tinkling of bells, the braying of beasts of burden, and the yelling of drovers. Mingled together, these cacophonous sounds keep coming closer. Hoca is frightened. He mumbles to himself: "I guess I came at a bad time. This sounds like Doomsday. I better get out and take a look." He quickly jumps out of the pit. By this time, the mules carrying crockery are just a few steps away. They get scared and start to kick and run. The loads on their backs fall off - and the crockery and the glassware come crashing down. The mule drivers grab Hoca and ask him what he is up to. "I am from the other world," says Hoca. "I'm out here taking a look at this world."

The drovers give Hoca a sound beating and leave him lying there black and blue. Then, they get hold of the mules, put the unbroken wares on their backs, and get going again.

When Hoca comes home with his head bashed, his eyes swollen, his hands and feet scratched, his wife asks: "What happened? What have they done to you?"

"I'm coming," Hoca says, "from the other world."

"You don't say," asks his wife again, "how are things in the other world?"

"Everything is just fine," Hoca replies, "so long as you don't frighten the mules carrying crockery."

## YOU'RE RIGHT TOO

Hoca is a judge. A plaintiff appears before him and presents his case. He asks: "I'm right, aren't I?"

Hoca responds: "You're right"

Then, the defendant tells his side of the story and Hoca says: "You're right." Hoca's wife who happens to be there is perplexed: "How could this be? You said they're both right. They can't both be right. Surely one of them is right and the other isn't..."

Hoca agrees: "My dear wife, you're right too."

## TAKE YOUR ABLUTION, GIVE ME MY SHOE

Hoca is performing his ablution in a brook. As he is washing his left foot to complete the ablution, what should he see: One of his shoes is floating away. He lunges forward to catch it, but he is forced to stop when the brook gets to be too deep. He stands there and stares after his shoe. He is so enraged by what the brook has done that he turns his fanny to it, breaks wind, and shouts:

"Take your ablution back and give me back my shoe."

Note: Breaking wind renders the ablution invalid.

## MOM WILL SHED TEARS

One of Hoca's two sons was making a living from his orchard and the other from earthenware jugs and pitchers. Hoca asked the first son how he was doing and the son said:

"This year I went whole hog and planted all sorts of things. If there's enough rain, just fine. But if it doesn't rain, Mom will shed tears for me."
Hoca went to his other son and asked how he was doing and the second son said:

"This year I mixed a lot of earth and water. If it doesn't rain, everything will be just fine. But if it rains, Mom will shed tears for me."
When Hoca came home, his wife asked how the boys were doing and he answered: "I don't know about the boys, but whether it rains or not, you're going to shed a lot of tears."

## HOW ABOUT THE STINK?

At a gathering, a man breaks wind with a bang. Then he scratches the floor with his foot so that the people there will think that was the noise. Hoca doesn't fall for it:

"All right," he says. "You faked the sound, but what do you do about the stink?"

## GOD'S SHARES, MAN'S SHARES

The boys of the neighborhood gather a lot of walnuts and ask Hoca to divide the walnuts among them. Hoca wants to know if they would rather have "God's shares or man's shares."

The boys say they prefer God's shares. So, Hoca gives some of them five walnuts, some ten, and another just one. The boys aren't pleased: "Hoca, what sort of God's shares are these?"

"That's the way," Hoca says, "God distributes - quite a lot to some, just a little to others, and none at all to still others."

Then the boys switch to "man's shares" and Hoca distributes the walnuts one by one so that each boy gets an equal number.

## WOLVES EAT UP THE DONKEY WHOSE MASTER IS DEAD

One winter day, Hoca goes up to the mountain to cut wood. It is bitter cold: His hands and feet are frozen. He mumbles to himself: "I think I'm dying... Maybe I'm dead," and he lies down. Right then, some wolves come and pounce on Hoca's donkey. Hoca turns his head and says to the wolves: "Go ahead and eat him up: Wolves eat up the donkey whose master is dead."

## BLINDMEN'S FIGHT

Blind beggars are lined up along the entrance to the mosque. Hoca happens to be passing by. He clinks the coins in his hand and says to the beggars: "Take all this money and split it among yourselves." Then he steps aside to watch.

The beggars begin to shout: "It's mine... He gave them to me... Don't take the purse... Let's have the pursue..." And they fight tooth and nail. Hoca muses: "So, this is how blindmen fight."

## WITH COLD CASH IN SIGHT, YOU CAN AFFORD TO LAUGH

One of Hoca's long-time creditors shows up one morning to demand his money.

"Don't worry," Hoca says. "Last night my wife and I came up with a scheme to pay you back. We're going to plant a hedge in front of our house. When herds of sheep go by, some of their wool will catch on the hedge. We'll collect the wool. My wife will spin it into yarn and I'll sell it at the bazaar. From the sale of this wool, we'll pay you every last penny we owe." Hearing this, the money-lender roars with laughter - and Hoca says to him: "You're a sly one, aren't you? When you see cold cash, you can afford to laugh."

## DO YOU BELIEVE THE DONKEY OR ME?

A neighbor asks Hoca for his donkey. Hoca is unwilling to lend the animal. Just as he says: "It isn't here: I sent it to the mill," the donkey is heard braying in the barn.

The neighbor is puzzled: "You said the donkey isn't here. There, it's braying, see." Hoca retorts: "You mean you don't believe me with my white beard and you believe the word of a donkey."

## I KNOW WHAT I'M GOING TO DO

At a village where he is staying as a guest, Hoca loses his saddlebag. He says to the villagers in the coffeehouse:

"You'd better find my saddlebag or else I know what I'm going to do!" This scares the daylights out of the villagers. The Headman exerts pressure on everybody. After an arduous search, the saddlebag is found. The Headman says:

"Hoca, you told us `... or else I know what I'm going to do. ' We've been wondering: What would you have done if we hadn't found your saddlebag?"

"Oh," says Hoca. "At home I have an old rug. I would have made another saddlebag out of that."

# BIG BLACK BOOK

Nasrettin Hoca is a judge. A man comes before him and says: "Your Honor, your cow gored and killed our cow."

"If," declares Hoca, "the owner of the cow that gored and killed is innocent, there is nothing to be done."

When the man hears Hoca's decision, he says: "Your Honor, I made a mistake. It's the other way around. The cow that got killed is yours and the one that killed it is ours."

"Is that so?" says Hoca. He calls the officer of the court and orders him: "Reach out to the top shelf and take down that big black book - let's take a look."

# LET THOSE WHO KNOW TELL THOSE WHO DON'T KNOW

Hoca mounts the pulpit and asks the congregation: "Do you know what I'm going to tell you?"

"How could we know?" responds the congregation. "We don't know."

Hoca says: "If you don't know, what's the use of my telling you?" And he leaves.

Another time, he goes up to the pulpit again and asks: "Do you know what I am going to tell you?"

This time, the congregation is prepared: "We know."

"If you already know," says Hoca, "why should I waste my breath?" He descends and leaves.

On another occasion, Hoca mounts the pulpit again and asks the same question.

The congregation gives him an answer which was agreed upon beforehand: "Some of us know, some of us don't know."

Whereupon Hoca says: "In that case, I will not waste your time. Let those who know tell those who don't know."

## YOU'RE INVITED TO MY FUNERAL PRAYERS

At a gathering, Hoca was complaining of Tamurlane's atrocities. Tamurlane himself happens to be there incognito. Hearing Hoca's invectives, he asks: "Aren't you overdoing it?" And he adds: "As far as I know, the man you're talking about isn't such a bad person."
Hoca is suspicious: "Where do you come from?"
"From Transoxiana."
Now Hoca becomes apprehensive: "Could you tell me your name?"
"Tamurlane."
His legs trembling, Hoca asks: "Is the title Sultan attached to that name?
"Yes. Sultan Tamurlane."
Hoca turns to the people there and says: "0, you Moslems, come, you're all invited to the funeral prayers for me."

## YOU ON THE INSIDE, ME FROM THE OUTSIDE

Hoca's donkey turns bad-tempered. So, he takes it to the marketplace and offers it for sale. The dealer praises the animal to high heaven: Potential buyers start bidding briskly. That's when Hoca realizes the worth of his donkey and runs up the bidding. Finally, the animal falls to Hoca's bid. Hoca pays the dealer and takes the donkey back home.
His wife is quite cheerful as she welcomes him. She tells him with great enthusiasm: "The yogurt-seller was going by. I asked him to give me two pounds. When he was looking the other way, I slipped my gold bracelet into the weight-side of the scale. So, he didn't notice that he was giving me a lot more than two pounds of yogurt."
Hoca sighs: "Honey, keep up the good work. With you working inside and me outside, we're going to make something of this family of ours."

# WHOEVER PAYS BLOWS THE WHISTLE

Hoca is on his way to the marketplace when children swarm around him clamoring "Get me a whistle! Buy me a whistle!" Only one of them gives Hoca money for a whistle.

In the evening Hoca returns and hands a whistle to the boy who had given him money. When the other children ask: "How about whistles for us?" Hoca replies: "The way it goes: Whoever pays, blows the whistle."

# YOU CAN'T CLOSE ANYBODY'S MOUTH TIGHT LIKE A BAG

Hoca is on his wag to the village. His son is riding the donkey and Hoca is walking. Passersby object: "Poor old man has to walk while the lad goes on the donkey. For shame! What's the world coming to?"

Overhearing this, Hoca tells his son to get down - and he mounts the donkey. Further ahead, some people sitting by the road complain: "Look at that big hunk of a man. He has no shame. He is riding the donkey and making that poor boy walk. People these days have no pity."

This time, Hoca asks his son to jump on the donkey. As the donkey is trudging on with the two riders, some villagers say to each other: "For goodness sake! Two men are riding that poor donkey. How cruel! The animal is a bag of bones, anyway. They're going to break its back."

When Hoca hears this, he dismounts and tells his son to get down. They go on their way, walking behind the donkey. As they approach the village, some people on the road make fun of them:

"Look at those stupid fools. Their donkey is trotting and those two are trudging along. They got no brains."

When he hears this last comment, Hoca says to his son:

"Did you hear that? It's best to go your own way. No matter what you do, people won't be satisfied. You can't close anybody's mouth tight like a bag."

## ONLY IF YOU'VE FALLEN OFF A ROOF, YOU'LL KNOW HOW I FEEL

Hoca falls off the roof of his house. Neighbors rush over asking him: "How're you feeling? Any aches and pains? Anything broken? Fractures?" Hoca says: "Is there anyone among you who has ever fallen off a roof? What's the use of my telling you? Only if you've fallen off a roof, you'll know how I feel."

## I HAD NO INTENTION OF MAKING A GO OF THE MARRIAGE; SO WHY SHOULD I LEARN HER NAME?

They ask Hoca: "What's your wife's name?"
He replies: "What do I know?"
Then they ask: "How long have you been married?"
"Twenty-five years," he says.
They are astonished: "Come now, how could a man be married for twenty-five years and not know his wife's name?"
Hoca replies: "I never intended to make a go of the marriage, so I never bothered to learn her name."

# DO AS YOU PLEASE

Hoca is walking through a graveyard when he suddenly sees a big dog pissing on a grave. He shouts: "Scram!" and threatens to chase the dog with his cudgel. But when the dog growls, showing all its sharp teeth, Hoca changes his tune:

"You're a good boy. Go ahead, do as you please."

# WHOEVER HAS THE BLUE BEAD

Hoca has two wives, both of whom frequently ask "Which one of us do you love more?" When he sees them separately, Hoca gives each wife a blue bead and tells her not to show it or mention it to the other wife or anyone else. One day, the two wives pursue the matter again: "Which one of us do you love more?"

Hoca replies: "The one who has the blue bead has my heart."

# EITHER YOU'VE NEVER HAD A BEATING OR YOU DON'T KNOW HOW TO COUNT

Tamurlane is furious at Nasrettin Hoca and orders his men to club him 1500 times.

Whereupon Hoca begins to laugh.

Tamurlane growls: "What are you laughing about?"

"Sire," says Hoca. "Either you've never had a beating or you don't know how to count."

## COMING HOME FROM A WEDDING

Hoca comes home in the evening - and what should he see? His wife is sulking.

"What's the matter this time?" he asks. "Can't you crack a smile? Why're you frowning?"

"I've just come back from a funeral," she explains. "That's why."

"That's fine, honey," replies Hoca. "But I've often seen how you come back from a wedding, too."

## LOOKS GOOD ON THE HUSSY

Hoca is preaching at the mosque, declaring that it is sinful for women to wear make-up. Someone in the audience points out that Hoca's wife wears make-up.

"But," says Hoca, "it looks good on the hussy."

## SO LONG AS YOU DON'T SHOW YOUR FACE TO ME

Hoca has an "arranged" marriage. According to the custom of that time, he sees the bride's face on the wedding night for the first time. She turns out to be ugly.

The following day, as they are going out together, she asks Hoca: "Tell me to whom I should show my face and to whom I shouldn't?" Hoca says: "You're welcome to show your face to anyone so long as you don't show it to me."

# A SELECTION OF NASRETTIN HOCA TALES

The Nasrettin Hoca books published until now have brought together 200-350 anecdotes. In the section that follows we are presenting a selection of the anecdotes we consider the best. We feel we must spell out the criteria which have guided our selection: As indicated in the foreword, The Nasrettin Hoca tales have been used and continue to be used as an apparatus by the Turkish people. The usefulness of these stories is often revealed in the resolution of a dilemma. The Hoca anecdotes provide a solution or a guidance to insoluble or intractable social problems by means of humor. In selecting the stories, we gave precedence to this aspect of the Nasrettin Hoca lore and used the yardstick of socially useful functions.

It would be relevant to explain this criterion with an example. According to some people, varying opinions held by the citizens of a country and their actions stemming from conflicting views constitute disorder or chaos: These people insist that everyone in the nation should think along the lines of a unitary doctrine which they hold beneficial - that everyone should act in accordance with it. In their view, order and equilibrium would be established by this kind of uniformity.

One of Hoca's very brief anecdotes serves to prove how fallacious this notion can be:

"Why," someone asks Hoca, "do some people go in one direction and some go another way?"

"Because," replies Hoca, "if we all went in the same direction, the world would lose its balance and topple."

This little Hoca story underlines the fact that equilibrium and order could be created not by uniformity of thought but rather through diversity - and thereby it serves a utilitarian social function.

Even the lengthiest accounts of the poverty and tribulation suffered by the Turkish peasant would fail to do justice to this topic compared to the following Hoca anecdote:

Hoca is plowing when suddenly a huge thorn pierces his foot. As he removes it, he mumbles:

"Thank goodness, I wasn't wearing the rawhide sandals I had bought last year:"

This early specimen of black humor demonstrates the limitless poverty of the Turkish peasant, thus serving a useful function.

In our opinion, this anecdote and some others like it have no usefulness in terms of their social function or substance An artificial social function could be forced upon such stories, but that would go against the grain of the Nasrettin Hoca lore. The fact remains, however, that stories of this type have been crammed into some Nasrettin Hoca books for the purpose of increasing the number of the stories.

In making our selection, we choose to leave out the stories which provide no solution to any issue and those without any social function or usefulness. It might be proper to site an example of how, in the real world, the Hoca tales can resolve a problem. At a Nasrettin Hoca Celebration held in his town (Akşehir), Prof. Fuat Köprülü the prominent historian of Turkish literature and a foreign Minister, made the statement that U.S. President Woodrow Wilson used to be very fond of a Hoca story. According to Köprülü, President Wilson himself had expressed his enthusiasm for this story and informed some journalists that he frequently told it.

At the end of World War I, President Wilson presented to the world his Fourteen Points which came to be known as "Wilson's Principles". It became clear to him, however, that his principles were disregarded. With the despondency he felt at that time, Wilson often told the following Nasrettin Hoca story:

One summer night, Hoca goes into his garden. He lifts the lid of the well and looks down: He is startled to see the moon at the bottom of the well. It bothers him that the moon has fallen all the way down. He, ties a big iron hook to a thick rope and lets it down hoping to pull the moon up. He begins to pull on the rope, but the hook gets stuck somewhere. Hoca pulls much harder - and all of a sudden the rope gets loose. Hoca falls flat on his back. He looks up - and sees that the moon is up in the sky where it belongs. He says to himself:

"Well, I fell flat on my back and hurt myself. But at least I've taken the moon out of the well and put it up there again."

Woodrow Wilson appreciated this story and told it repeatedly, because it brought a solution to one of the major problems confronting him. Just as Hoca was striving to pull the moon out of the well, President Wilson had expounded various principles to save the peace. But his idealism was not in tune with the realities which stayed put just as the moon remained in its place in the sky. Consequently, nothing was really saved - and the Hoca story resolved a problem which corresponded to Wilson's mood. The abovementioned considerations constitute the criteria we have followed in selecting the Hoca stories featured in this Section.

Hoca borrows his neighbor's cauldron and when he returns it he puts a small pot into it. The neighbor wonders what it's all about.

"Your cauldron," Hoca replies, "was pregnant, it turns out. That's the baby."
Later Hoca borrows the cauldron again. But many days go by and Hoca does not return it. Finally the neighbor asks for it. With a sad expression, Hoca says:

"My condolences. Your cauldron is dead."
"Come on, Hoca," says the neighbor. "How could a cauldron die?"
"My dear neighbor," Hoca retorts. "You had no doubt that it gave birth, yet you doubt if it died!"

Out in the meadow, Hoca manages to catch a rabbit. He throws it into his bag and closes the bag tight. Planning to show it to his friends and neighbors, he invites them to his home that night: "I'm going to show you something amazing."

His wife is curious about what the bag contains. When she opens the bag, the rabbit gets away. In order to conceal the fact that the bag was opened and the rabbit ran away, she stuffs the barley-scale into the bag and returns the bag to its previous place.

When friends and neighbors are gathered, Hoca brings the bag, places it right in the middle, opens it with great care - and the scale falls out of it. Everyone is stunned, but Hoca says without losing his composure:

"Here you are: If you fill this measure ten times, it adds up to one bushel."

Hoca had two wives who were jealous of each other. Whenever they asked which wife he liked better, Hoca would say he loved both of them.

One day, the younger wife asked: "Suppose we are in a rowboat on Lake Akşehir. The boat capsizes and we both fall into the lake. Which one of us would you rescue?"

Hoca turned to his older wife and said:

"I think you're a bit of a swimmer, aren't you?"

There is a ban against carrying weapons. The police chief catches Hoca bearing a forked dagger.

"Hoca," he asks, "Don't you know it is forbidden to bear weapons? What are you doing with that huge dagger?"

"That's no weapon," Hoca explains "There are errors in some books. I make corrections with this."

"Come off it, Hoca," says the police chief. "How could anyone scratch errors in books with an enormous dagger like that?"

Hoca chuckles: "Some books have such huge errors that even this enormous dagger is too small to correct them."

Hoca asks his friends to have him buried upside down when he dies. They ask him why. "Because," he replies. "When the end of the world comes, everything will be topsy turvy and everyone will be upended - and I'll be the only one to come out the right way up."

Hoca asks a friend: "How does one know when somebody is dead?"
"His friend explains: "His hands and feet turn cold, ice-cold."
A few days later, Hoca goes up to the mountain to chop wood. It's a terribly cold day: His hands and feet turn cold, ice-cold. He remembers what his friend had told him: Thinking he's dead, he lies on the ground. He waits for some time for people to remove him and bury him. But no one shows up. So, he rises to his feet. Trudging with great difficulty, he comes home. His wife opens the door. Hoca says to her:
"I was up there on the mountain - and I died. Let our friends and neighbors know and ask them to arrange my funeral." Then, he goes back to the mountain.
His wife breaks into tears. She tears her hair out desperately. She goes from neighbor to neighbor crying: "My husband died up on the mountain!"
Some of the neighbors wonder: "If he died up on the mountain, who brought you the news?"
Hoca's wife explains: "Poor soul had nobody... He died by himself and he came home himself to deliver the news."

Hoca dreams that someone hands him nine gold coins. But he insists he must have ten. Suddenly he wakes up and sees that there is nothing in his hand. He shuts his eyes again and stretches out his hand.

"OK, have it your way," he says. "I'll settle for nine."

Whatever Hoca says, his son does the opposite.

One day, father and son grind their wheat at the mill, load the flour sacks on the donkey, and take the road back to their village. Hoca crosses a stream and then looks back - and notices that the sacks are sagging down too much on the right side of the donkey. His son, who is holding the halter isn't aware that anything is wrong. Hoca knows that if he were to ask his son to adjust the sacks on the right he would do the exact opposite. He decides to tell his son the opposite so that he would adjust the right side:

"Son, the sacks on the left are, sagging. Adjust them so that they won't fall off."

The son thinks that, this time, he should do exactly what his father tells him to do. He fixes the left side - and the load loses its balance and falls into the stream.

"Son of a gun," Hoca says. "Once in forty years you listened to what your father told you - and on that one occasion you deprived us a whole winter's supply of flour."

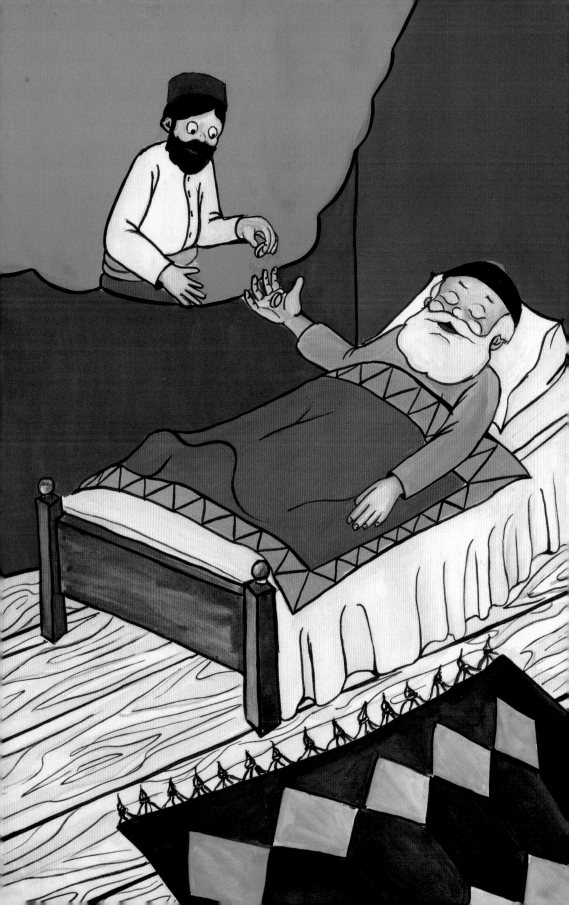

A poor man shows up at Hoca's house. To be given hospitality, he presents himself as "a guest sent by God".
Hoca points to the mosque across the street and says:
"You've come to the wrong place. That, over there, is God's house."

Hoca and his wife are in bed at night. She says: "How about moving over a bit?"
Hoca gets out of the bed, gets dressed, goes out, and starts walking. He walks until daybreak when he runs into an acquaintance who asks:
"Where are you heading, Hoca?"
"I don't know how far I'll go," says Hoca. "I'll wait here. You go ask my wife and let me
know: Should I keep moving over?"

Hoca stuffs peaches into his pockets and says:
"To anyone who can guess what I have in my pockets, I'll give all the peaches."
All the people there guess: "Peaches..."
"My goodness," Hoca says: "It's impossible to hide anything from you people."

Hoca is plowing when suddenly a huge thorn pierces his foot. As he removes it, he mumbles:
"Thank goodness, I wasn't wearing the rawhide sandals I had bought last year."

The people of Akşehir have been suffering terribly at the hands of tamurlane. One day Hoca goes to Tamurlane and 'asks:
"Are you going to get out of this town or not?"
Tamurlane is furious: "I'm not going to leave!"
Hoca says to him: "If you're not leaving, I know what I'm going to do."
Tamurlane screams at him: "What do you think you can do?" "Nothing much," says Hoca. "If you're not going to get out, I'll take the people of the town and get out myself."

Someone says to Hoca: "Your wife is out all the time. She keeps visiting all the houses in the neighborhood."
"I don't believe it," says Hoca. "If that were true, she would drop in at our house too."

Hoca falls off his donkey. When children laugh at him, he says: "Why are you laughing? - I was going to get off anyway."

A foreign scientist shows up in Akşehir. He asks for the wisest man in town. The townspeople recommend Hoca.

The visiting scientist wants to put Hoca through a test. He draws a circle on the ground with the stick in his hand.

Hoca, too, has a stick in his hand. He draws a straight line dividing the circle into two. The scientist draws another line cutting the circle into four slices. Then Hoca, using sign language, makes believe he'll take three slices and give one slice to the scientist.

The foreigner holds both his hands down and shakes his fingers. To respond to this, Hoca turns his hands up and does the opposite of what the visiting scientist has just done.

Thereupon, the scientist shakes Hoca's hand and warmly congratulates him. The onlookers are baffled. They ask the scientist to tell them what's been happening, and he explains:

"By drawing a circle, I asked him: 'They claim the world is round. What is your opinion?' Hoca drew a line right through the middle telling me: 'Certainly the world is round and the Equator goes right through the middle of it.' I then divided the circle into four parts and asked him what this signifies. He set three parts aside indicating that Three-fourths of the world is sea and one-fourth land.' Then I held my hands down and shook my fingers. That was a question about the cause of rain. He held his hands up with his fingers pointing to the sky which was his way of telling me: 'Vapor rises from the earth and that's how it happens.' Your Hoca knows everything."

The people then go to Hoca and ask him. He gives them his version:

"This is some greedy guy. He drew before me a circle, that is to say, a tray of baklava. I drew a line through the middle saying `You can't have all the baklava. You take half and I'll take the other half.' He then divided the circle into four. I claimed three parts: Three-fourths is for me and a quarter for you.' He shook his fingers over the baklava: He was asking me if we should sprinkle ground filberts and nuts on it. I raised my fingers to suggest that may be we should put it into a red-hot oven. Whatever that man drew, I was able to catch his meaning. Finally we gave up."

One day, Hoca, brandishing a stick, chases his wife into the street. He keeps screaming:

"Don't stop me. Let me kill her!"

People who hear the screams run and stop the fight. The men take Hoca into one house and the women take his wife into another house. In the house they take Hoca to, a wedding party is going on. When the baklava tray is brought in, Hoca gobbles up the pieces in front of him - and then, saying "If I had been able to catch her, I would've turned her around..." he turns the tray to his side so that he can have more baklava.

The people at the wedding are curious: "Hoca, you had never done anything like this. What was the reason for the fight?"

While gobbling up big chunks of baklava, Hoca explains: "My wife and I started to talk about why we had not been intived to this wedding. Our talk turned into a row which gradually became harsh - and we ended up swinging punches."

Hoca takes his donkey to the marketplace to sell it. Prospective buyers gather together. When somebody touches the tail, the donkey kicks the man. Someone else puts his hand on the rump: it kicks him with both of his hind feet. And when one of the men tries to look at his teeth, it bites him. Shocked, the auctioneer says to Hoca:

"You just won't be able to sell this beast. No one will buy it. You'd better take it away."

Hoca replies: "I didn't bring it here to sell it anyway. I brought it here so that everyone would see what an awful creature it is and how I've been suffering because of its bad temper."

Hoca goes to a bath dressed shabbily. The attendants likewise treat him shabbily and give him a tattered towel. After bathing, Hoca hands the attendants 10 coins as tip. They are dumbfounded at this generous tip. Some time later, Hoca goes to the same bath. This time the attendants give him the royal treatment. After bathing, Hoca leaves a tip of one coin. He says to the astounded attendants:

"Last time I paid you the tip for this time; the tip I give you now is for last time."

Someone cautions Hoca that his wife never stays home and goes from house to house in the neighborhood. He suggests Hoca should warn

"Sure," says Hoca. "If I run into her, I'll tell her."

From the horse-block, Hoca mounts a horse the wrong way. Some people there start shouting:

"You mounted the horse wrong way."

"Nothing of the sort," Hoca shouts back. "I didn't get up the wrong way. The horse is left-handed: It came up to the horse-block the wrong way."

Somebody who was about to perform his ablution in Lake Akşehir asks Hoca:
"While washing, which way should I look?"
Hoca replies: "Where you have your clothes."

## JUST AS HE WAS GETTING USED TO IT

A protracted winter reduces the amount of the barley available for Hoca's donkey. So, Hoca gradually cuts down on the barley with which he feeds his donkey: There is less from one day to the next. And then he feeds the donkey once every two or three days. What should he see when he enters the barn one day: The donkey is dead.
"Pity!" mumbles Hoca. "Just as he was getting used to it, he died."

Hoca is winding his turban, but fails to link the tip to the back of the turban no matter how much he tries. He gets so irritated that he decides to take the turban to the bazaar and sell it there. Bidding starts at the bazaar. A prospective buyer bids so high that
Hoca warns him:
"Look here, brother. Don't bid so high, because when you try to wind this turban, the tip just doesn't link with the back."

Hoca goes into a shop to buy baggy trousers. He makes his selection. They bargain and agree on a price. Right then, he fancies a cloak which is priced exactly the same. So, Hoca says:
"I decided I'm not going to buy the baggy trousers. Sell me the cloak instead." The salesman wraps the cloak and hands the package to Hoca. As Hoca is leaving the shop with the package, the salesman reminds him: "You didn't pay for the cloak."
"What do you mean?" says Hoca. "Didn't I leave the trousers for it?"
The salesman reminds Hoca:
"But you never paid for the trousers."
"For God's sake," Hoca says. "Since I didn't buy the trousers, why should I pay for them?"

A man slaps Hoca as hard as he can and then apologizes: "Forgive me, I made a mistake. I thought you were a friend of mine." But Hoca takes the man to court. The judge knows the defendant well and hands down a very lenient decision:
"The fine for a slap is one coin. If you have a coin on you, hand it to Hoca. If not, go home and bring it here." The man goes home.
Hoca waits for a long time, but there is no sight of the man. Hoca jumps to his feet, slaps the judge as hard as he can, and leaves saying:
"When he brings the coin, you take it."

Hoca is having roast chicken. Somebody says:
"That chicken looks great. Would you give me some?"
Hoca answers: "It isn't mine to give. It belongs to my wife."
The man challenges him: "That may be so, but you are eating it."
"What can I do?" replies Hoca. "My wife ordered me to eat it when she gave it to me. So I'm eating it."

On a moonlit night, Hoca sees in his backyard a white figure. Thinking it might be a burglar, he asks his wife to hand him the bow and an arrow. He takes aim and lets the arrow fly through. Right on target.

He waits untie daybreak to go into the backyard. He is shocked to see that what he thought was a burglar is his own cloak that his wife washed and hung on the clothesline.

He kneels and repeatedly says: "Thank God! Thank God!" His wife asks: "Why are you thanking God?"

"Sure I have to thank God," Hoca replies. "I managed to strike right in the middle. Just imagine what would have happened if I were in it."

Hoca stops in the middle of the street and has a long chat with a man. As they are about to go their separate ways, he says to the man:

"Forgive me, but I have no idea who you are."

"In that case, why have you been talking to me as if we've been friends all our lives?"

"I took a look: Your robe is the same as mine, so is your turban. I thought you were me."

One of Hoca's neighbors dies. As the coffin is being taken out of his house, the widow is heard weeping and crying out: "Oh, my only one, where are you going? At the place you're heading there's neither light nor water... there's neither fire nor hearth..."

When Hoca hears these screams, he says to his wife:

"Run along and shut the door tight. They're bringing the coffin to our house."

## KEEPING BUSY

Hoca finds himself without a job. His friends advise him to occupy himself with something. Hoca decides to sell eggs. He buys nine eggs for one coin and sells ten for one coin.

When his friends ask: "What sort of trading is this?" he explains:

"It's better than being idle. Let my friends see I'm busy buying and selling."

Unbeknownst to everybody, Hoca saves money for all sorts of emergency. He tries to find a safe place to hide his savings: First he buries the money in the garden, but then takes it out, because he is afraid it might not be safe enough. He hides it somewhere
in the house, but that too strikes him as too risky. Finally, he decides to tie his purse to the tip of a, pole - and he sticks the pole into a small mound in his garden. He figures that no one would imagine there might be money on the tip of a pole. Besides, even if someone might imagine that, it would take a bird to snatch the purse from up there.

While Hoca comtemplates all this, a man has been spying on him. When hoca ties the purse to the pole and erects the pole and then leaves, the man takes the pole down, removes the purse, puts some dung on the tip, and sets it up again.

Some tim later, Hoca needs some money: He takes the pole down and sees that the purse is gone. He is flabbergasted that there is dung instead. He mumbles to himself:

"God Almighty! I said to myself no man can go up there. How, then, did an ox manage to go all the way up?"

Hoca owes the grocer a lot of money. The grocer is a tactless man who often demands payment in the presence of others. Hoca asks him:

"How much do I owe you?"

"Twenty-five coins."

"And how about the preacher?"

"Twenty-four coins."

"You know," says Hoca. "The preacher is a close friend of mine. We're the best of friends. Now, I owe you twenty-five. When the preacher pays you the twenty-four that he owes you, the unpaid balance is one, right? Aren't you ashamed to make these demands on me in the company of others for one measly coin?"

Hoca often brags in Tamurlane's presence that he is a superb archer and he never misses a shot. One day, Tamurlane challenges him:

"Come, Hoca, let's give it a try."

The target is propped up. Hoca takes quite a few steps backward, pulls the bow and shoots an arrow: It sails past the target. Without losing his composure, Hoca declares:

"There - that's the way the Royal Chief Archer shoots an arrow."

He looses another arrow and this one goes even wider off the mark. Hoca is unflappable:

"This is the way our Police Chief shoots an arrow."

Third time around, by a fluke, the arrow lands right on target: bull's eye. Puffed up with pride, Hoca turns to Tamurlane and announces:

"There you are, Sire, this is the way Nasrettin Hoca practices archery."

Hoca has a serious illness. He is bed-ridden. When he realizes that he is in a critical condition, he calls his wife to his bedside:

"Honey," he says. "Go, do yourself up, put some perfume on, jewelry too. Make yourself pretty. Wear your Sunday best. Then come and sit right here." His wife objects: "How could I dress up and make up when you're in this codition?" Hoca insists. His wife wants to find out why.

"When the Angel of Death comes," Hoca explains, "and sees you dressed to the teeth, looking radiant, maybe he'll like you or even fall in love with you and take you away instead of me."

Tamurlane turns one of his male elephants over to the people of Akşehir ordering them to take care of it. In addition to wreaking havoc in the town, the elephant becomes a terrible burden on the people who are too poor to get decent food for themselves. A group of them visits Hoca with a request: "Please ask Tamurlane to take the monster back."

Hoca says: "Form a committee. Let's all go together. I'll serve as your spokesman."

A committee is formed of about fifteen prominent citizens of Akşehir. Hoca joins them. And they set out. But since these people are terrified of Tamurlane, they vanish one by one. Each one has an excuse: "I've got to pass water," "I've forgotten my tobacco-box at home," etc.

Assuming that the committee is right behind him, Hoca briskly walks into Tamurlane's tent and begins to make his plea: "Sire, the people of our town..." He turns back a little to point them out - and suddenly realizes that not one of them came into the tent. Since he had started making his plea, he continues:

"The people of our town are so happy with the male elephant... They are happy beyond words. But there is a slight problem: The animal is lonesome and unhappy. We would like your Majesty to consider giving the people of the town a female elephant as a companion for him."

Tamurlane is overjoyed to hear this plea. "All right," he says. "I shall do what the people wish - as soon as possible."

Hoca goes back to town. People gather round him asking him anxiously: "Please tell us, Hoca, what happened?"

"I have great news for you," beams Hoca. "To keep the male calamity company, a female calamity will soon arrive. Now you can rejoice."

Hoca is riding his donkey, his sack on his back. He runs into friends who ask him why he is carrying the sack himself. Hoca explains:
"This poor animal has a big enough burden carrying me. How can I put the sack on him too? To spare him, I have the sack on my back."

A feudal lord who had suffered a great deal at the hands of women goes around asking people what they think of women. He orders the beheading of anyone who speaks in favor of women. One day, he confronts Hoca:
"Are you married?"
Hoca responds by saying: "How could any man remain a bachelor until my age?"
The lord is so furious he foams at the mouth. He bellows: "Behead him!"
Hoca realizes he is serious and makes a last-ditch effort: "Don't rush to judgement, my lord. Why don't you ask me if I divorced my first wife and got married again?
Or if, in addition to my first wife, I brought home a second wife. Or if my first wife died and soon I married someone? That is to say, my lord, why don't you ask me if I didnt come to my senses after the first stupid foolish thing I did and went ahead and did the same stupid foolish thing all over again. No. I made this stupid foolish mistake just once. You know best, my lord, but one doesn't cut off the head of a horse after it stumbles once."
The feudal lord likes what Hoca says and he pardons him.

One summer night, Hoca goes into his garden. He lifts the lid of the well and looks down: He is startled to see the moon at the bottom of the well. It bothers him that the moon has fallen all the way down. He ties a big iron hook to a thick rope and lets it down hoping to pull the moon up. He begins to pull on the rope, but the hook gets stuck somewhere. Hoca pulls much harder -and all of a sudden the rope gets loose. Hoca falls flat on his back. He looks up - and sees the moon up in the sky where it belongs. He says to himself:

"Well, I fell flat on my back and hurt myself. But at least I've taken the moon out of the well and put it up there again."

Hoca stuffs peaches into his pockets and says:

"To anyone who can guess what I have in my pockets, I'll give all the peaches."
All the people there guess: "Peaches..."
"My goodness," Hoca says: "It's impossible to hide anything from you people."

Hoca is digging a big hole in his backyard. His neighbor asks: "What're you doing?"

"A few days ago," Hoca explains, "I was repairing the house. Quite a bit of rubble came out. I'm going to bury all that in this hole."

The neighbor asks again: "Well, what do you plan to do with the dirt that comes out of the hole you're digging?"

Hoca says: "I'll dig another hole and stuff the dirt in it."

"All right," says the neighbor. "What are you going to do with the dirt from the second hole?"

"Come on," replies Hoca. "You can't expect me to know every last detail."

Someone who listens to Hoca's sermon jokes:

"They say your donkey is a judge, is that true?"

"That's correct," Hoca retorts. "When I preach, the beast props its ears and listens so intently."

A neighbor hears a tremendous racket in Hoca's house at night. He rushes over there and taps on the door. Hoca opens the door. The neighbor asks him:

"Just a short while ago, I heard a terrible noise here. What happened?"

"Oh, nothing," Hoca answers. "My wife threw my cloak down the stairs... that's all."

The neighbor doesn't go for the story: "Come on, Hoca, how can a cloak make all that racket?"

"Cut it out neighbor," Hoca says. "I just happened to be in it."

From the horse-block, Hoca mounts a horse the wrong way. Some people there start shouting:

"You mounted the horse wrong way."

"Nothing of the sort," Hoca shouts back. "I didn't get up the wrong way. The horse is left-handed: It came up to the horse-block the wrong way."

Hoca is looking for something in the pantry when a sieve falls on his head. It then falls on the floor and bounces up to hit his head again. Furious, Hoca kicks the sieve as hard as he can. It goes flying against the wall and comes back, this time striking Hoca on the shoulder. Hoca gives one more ferocious kick up to the ceiling: The sieve bounces back from the ceiling and lands on Hoca's knees.

Realizing that he won't be able to win the fight, Hoca gives up struggling with the sieve. He draws his knife and shouts: "If you're a brave man, come out now!"

Hoca and Tamurlane are bathing in a public bath. Tamurlane asks: "If I were a serf for sale, what price would you be willing to pay for me?"

Hoca says: "Two coins."

"Be fair," says Tamurlane. "My towel here alone is worth two coins."

"Well," replies Hoca. "It was the towel's worth that I had in my mind."

After the death of Hoca's wife, his friends arrange for him to marry a widow. When they go to bed at night, the woman keeps telling Hoca about her first husband. One night, Hoca can no longer take it. He kicks her out of the bed right on to the floor. Next day, she goes to her father and complains. The father takes the matter up with Hoca who explains:

"You see, we have a small bed. Me, my deceased wife, my new wife, and her first husband - all four of us didn't fit the bed - and I guess your daughter fell off."

## WHOEVER HAS THE BLUE BEAD

Hoca has two wives, both of whom frequently ask "Which one of us do you love more?" When he sees them separately, Hoca gives each wife a blue bead and tells her not to show it or mention it to the other wife or anyone else. One day, the two wives pursue the matter again: "Which one of us do you love more?"

Hoca replies: "The one who has the blue bead has my heart."

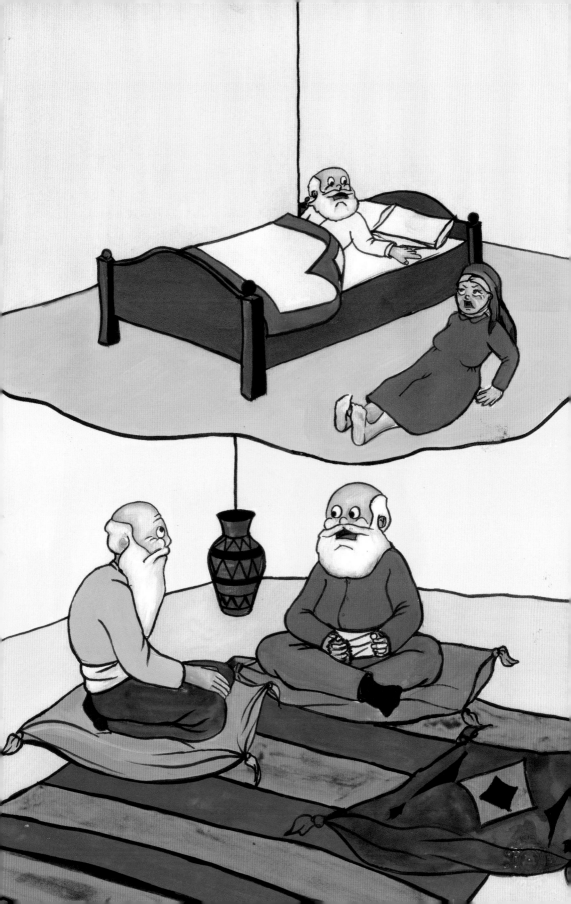

Hoca and his friends are having a picnic by Lake Akşehir one summer day. As they are having fun, suddenly they see that a man falls into the Lake. He is bobbing up and down. His hand comes out and he is heard shouting "Save me! Rush!" The men lined up on the shore keep saying to him: "Give me your hand! Give us your hand!"

But the man just does not give them his hand. When he is on the verge of drowning, Hoca shouts to him from the shore: "Take my hand! Go ahead, take my hand!"

And the man, right then when he is drowning, takes Hoca's hand and goes up on the shore.

Everybody is curious: "Hoca, why didn't he hold our hands and he held yours?"

Hoca explains: "This man is a loan-shark. He never gives; he only takes. He wouldn't give you his hand, because you said give us your hand. But I said to him take my hand. So, he immediately grabbed my hand."

Hoca and his wife are in bed at night. She says: "How about moving over a bit?"

Hoca gets out of the bed, gets dressed, goes out, and starts walking. He walks until daybreak when he runs into an acquaintance who asks:

"Where are you heading, Hoca?"

"I don't know how far I'll go," says Hoca. "I'll wait here. You go ask my wife and let me

know: Should I keep moving over?"

People were debating if anyone could go up to the top of a tall tree. Hoca challenged them:
"If I can do it, you pay me one coin each. If I can't, I'll pay you one coin each"
The bet is on. Then, Hoca says:
"Bring me a tall ladder."
The others object: "There was nothing in our bargain about a ladder."
"All right," retorts Hoca. "Was there any mention of my going up there without a ladder?"
And he pockets all the coins.

"Why," someone asks Hoca, "do some people go in one direction and some go another way?"
"Because,".replies Hoca, "if we all went in the same direction, the world would lose its balance and topple.

## JUST SUPPOSE

Hoca sits by Lake Akşehir throwing yogurt culture into it. Someone passing by is astonished:

"Whar are you doing Hoca?"

"Putting yogurt culture into the lake," Hoca replies

The man is perplexed: "How can a lake turn into yogurt?"

"I know," says Hoca. "It can't, it won't. But just suppose it does..."

Hoca and his wife are at the dinner table. She serves the soup and takes a spoonful before Hoca does. The soup is so hot that it scalds her mouth and tears rush into her eyes. Hoca asks:

"Why are you shedding tears?"

"Oh," she replies. "My late father used to be so fond of this soup. I remembered that: That's why I'm crying."

"May he rest in peace," Hoca says. "He's gone. No use crying your eyes out." Then he has some soup - and it's as if his mouth is on fire and tears begin to roll down his cheeks. His wife says:

"I cried, because I remembered my father. What are you crying about?"

"I'm crying, because your father, that scoundrel is dead, and a disgrace like you is still alive."

# MAYBE THERE IS A ROAD AT THE TOP OF THE TREE

A bunch of boys who see Hoca approaching decide to play a trick on him: They will wager that no one can climb a nearby tree and if Hoca falls for it and claims he can climb, they will take his shoes when he goes up and they will run away.

When Hoca comes along, they say to him: "We were just talking that no one could climb this tree here. What do you think, Hoca?"

Hoca says: "I can climb it."

"Let's see you do it, then."

Hoca takes his shoes off, sticks them into his shirt, and begins to climb.

The boys are alarmed: "Hoca, why are you taking your shoes with you?"

"You never can tell," says Hoca. "Maybe there's a road at the top of the tree."

Hoca says: "For a long time I've been longing for halvah, but it just proves impossible to have some made."

"Why?" his friends ask.

Hoca explains: "There is butter but no flour. They get butter and flour, this time there's no sugar. Then they find all the ingredients, but I am not available."

# I KNOW HOW YOU WERE IN YOUR YOUTH

Hoca tries to mount a horse which proves too tall for him. Just in case some people may have seen him, he exclaims: "You
should have seen me in my youth!"
When he realizes that there is no one nearby, he mutters to
himself:
"Rubbish. I know how you were in your youth, too."

The police superintendent, who is an extremely stingy man, asks Hoca to give him a greyhound with a lean belly. Hoca finds a big stray dog, puts a lash around his neck, and takes it to the superintendent.
"Look, Hoca,." says the superintendent. "I asked you to get me a greyhound with a lean belly. Instead, you brought me a huge sheep dog - a mongrel at that."
"Don't worry," Hoca replies. "If it stays with you one month, this enormous dog will turn into a lean greyhound."

Hoca stops in the middle of the street and has a long chat with a man. As they are about to go their separate ways, he says to the man:
"Forgive me, but I have no idea who you are."
"In that case, why have you been talking to me as if we've been friends all our lives?"
"I took a look: Your robe is the same as mine, so is your turban. I thought you were me."

Hoca conceals his neighbor's goose under his cloak and takes to the road. Midway, he opens his cloak up just a little to see how the goose is doing - and the goose sticks its head out and hisses "Tsssss..."
"There." Hoca exclaims. "That's exactly what I was about to tell you."

## SELECTED BIBLIOGRAPHY

- **ABACI,** Tahir. Nasreddin Hoca. Doyuran Ofset, İstanbul, 1980 (Illustrated)
- **ADALI,** Kutlu. Nasreddin Hoca ve Kıbrıs. (Nasreddin Hodja and Cyprus). Lefkoşe, 1971.
- **AHISKALI,** Yusuf. Nasreddin Hoca. Mete Matbaası, İstanbul 1965.
- **AHISKALI,** Yusuf. Şiirle Nasrettin Hoca. (Nasreddin Hodja with Poems). Mete Basımevi, İstanbul, 1965. (Illustrated)
- **AK,** Vedat. Resimli Fotoğraflı Nasreddin Hoca Fıkraları. (Illustrated Tales of Nasreddin Hodja). Uyanış Basımevi, Akşehir, 1967.
- **AKAY,** M. Samim. Nasreddin Hoca. Ayyıldız Kitabevi, İstanbul, 1959. (Illustrated)
- **AKGÜLLÜ,** Önder. Resimli ve Seçilmiş Nasreddin Hoca Fıkraları. (Illustrated and Selected Tales of Nasreddin Hodja). Yıldız Kitabevi, İstanbul, 1970.
- **AKSOY,** Mehmet Ali. Nasreddin Hoca. Semih Lütfi Kitabevi, İstanbul, 1958.
- **ALINMAZ,** Halil. Resimli ve Seçilmiş Nasreddin Hoca Fıkraları. (Illustrated and Seleceted Tales of Nasreddin Hodja). Yıldız Kitabevi, İstanbul, 1973.
- **ALİ NURİ,** Nasreddin Khodjas schwanke and streiche TOrkische Geschichten aus Timurlenks Tagen. Verlagsbuch handlung. Kanaat, İstanbul, 1932. (Illustrated)
- **ARRATOON,** Nicolas. Gems of Oriental Wit and Humour and the Sayings of Molla Nasreddin. Kalküta, 1894.
- **ASAF,** M. . Nasreddin Hoca, En Tuhaf Sözleri, Latifeleri ve Hikayeleri. (Most Amusing Tales of Nasreddin Hodja). Yeni Sark Kitabevi, İstanbul, 1940. (Illustrated)
- **BABLER,** Otto F. . Nasreddin Hoca. İz Zbornika za narodni jivot: obiçaye yujnih Slavena. Zagreb, 1934.
- **BAKER,** William Burchhardt. Pleasing Tales of Khoja Nasr-id-deen Efendi. London, 1854.
- **BARNHAM,** Henry Dudley. The Khoja: Tales of Nasr-ed-din. Appleton, New York, 1924. (Illustrated)
- **BARROW,** George. The Turkish Jester or the Pleasantries of Cogia Nasreddin Efendi. Ipswich, 1884.
- **BATU,** Hamit. Nasreddin Hodja. L'humour Philosophique. Ajans Türk Matbaası, Ankara, 1974
- **BEDIÇKIAN,** C.V. Turkish Gems or the Tales of My Childhood Being the Funny Sayings and Doings of Nasreddin Hodja, The Turkish Esop. Alleghany, 1896.
- **BİRAND,** Mehmet Ali. Les Anecdotes de Nasreddin Hodja. İstanbul. (Illustrated)
- **BİRAND,** Mehmet Ali. Stories of Hodja with Colored Pictures. İstanbul.
- **BOJINOV,** Ivan K.. Nastradin Hodja, hitrini smehotvorsvo, anekdoti i pr. Sofya, 1909.
- **BOLAYIR,** Enver. Resimli Nasreddin Hoca Fıkraları. (Illustrated Tales of Nasreddin 97 Nadia). Kültür Kitabevi, İstanbul, 1979.
- **BÖÖK,** Frederic. Nasreddin Hodscha Turkischa sagor Och. Skamt Historier. Atergivna och Inledda. Söners Förlag, Stockholm, 1928.
- **BURDURLU,** İbrahim Zeki. Ömürsün Nasreddin Hocam. (My Funny Hodja). Karınca Matbaacılık Koll. Şti., İzmir, 1965.
- **BÜYÜK** Nasreddin Hoca. (The Great Nadia). Maarif Kitaphanesi, İstanbul, 1959. (Illustrated)
- **CAMERLOHER** und Prelog. Meister Nasr-eddin's schwanke und Rauber und Richter. Trieste, 1857.
- **CAMİLİOĞLU,** Mithat. Nasreddin Hoca Fıkraları. (Tales of Nasreddin Hodja). Küçük Karınca Yayınları, İstanbul, 1983.
- **CANDAŞ,** Ömür. Nasreddin Hoca, En Büyük Güldürü Ustamızın En Ünlü Fıkraları (Most Famous Anecdotes of Nasreddin Hodja). Ya-Ba Yayınları, İstanbul, 1978. (Illustrated)
- **CHIROL,** Valantin. Tales of Nasreddin Hodja. London, 1923.
- **CUMBUL,** Sadi. Nasreddin Hoca. Nasreddin Hoca Derneği Yayınları, Akşehir, 1964.
- **DAENECKE,** Eric. More Tales of Mullah Nasirud-din. Exposition Press, New York, 1961.
- **DECOURDEMANCHE,** J.A.. Les plaisanteries de Nasr-Eddin Hodja. Paris, 1876.
- **DECOURDEMANCHE,** J.A.. Sottisier de Nasr-Eddin Hodja, Bouffon de Tamerlan, suivi d'autres faceties turques, traduits sur des manuscrits inedits. Gay et Douce, Bruxelles, 1878.
- **DİLİBAL,** Hilmi. Hoca ve Eşeği. (Hodja and His Donkey). Ayyıldız Matbaası, İstanbul, 1980. (Illustrated)
- **DINESCU,** V. Din ispravile lui Nasredin Hogea. Editura Tineretului, Bucureşti, 1961. (Other Editions 1968, 1971)
- **DOWNING,** Charles. Tales of the Hodja. Oxford University Press, London, 1964. (Illustrated)
- **DOYURAN,** Enver. Büyük Nasreddin Hoca Latifeleri. (Great Jokes of Nasreddin Hodja). Sağlam Kitabevi, İstanbul, 1977. (Illustrated)
- **DOYURAN,** Enver. Resimli Nasreddin Hoca Latifeleri. (Illustrated Tales of Nasreddin Hodja). Aka Kitabevi, İstanbul, 1961. (Other Editions 1967, 1975, 1977, 1983)
- **DRAGOMANON.** Nasr-Eddin Anecdotes. Klevskaya Starina, Ukrayna, 1889.
- **ERCAN,** Hakkı Resimli Nasreddin Hoca Fıkraları. (Illustrated Tales of Nasreddin Hodja). Rafet Zaimler Yayınevi, İstanbul, 1954.
- **ERCAN,** Hakkı. Nasreddin Hoca'dan Fıkralar. (Tales From Nasreddin Hodja). Aka Kitabevi, İstanbul, 1961. (Other Editions 1967, 1975, 1977, 1983)
- **ERGİNER,** Kaya. Nasreddin Hoca, Tarihi ve Hikayelerinin Anlamı. (Historical Personality of the Hodja and the Sense of His Tales). Gün Matbaası, İstanbul, 1969.
- **ERGÜN,** Sami. Manzum Nasreddin Hoca Fıkraları ve Hikayeleri. (Stories of Nasreddin Hodja In Verse). Milli Eğitim Basımevi, Ankara, 1950. (Illustrated)
- **ERGÜN,** Ayhan. Nasreddin Hoca. Örgün Yayınları İstanbul, 1983.
- **FELEK,** Burhan. Nasreddin Hoca. Milliyet Yayınları, İstanbul, 1982.
- **FELEK,** Burhan. Nasreddin Hoca. Milliyet Yayınları, İstanbul, 1983. (Illustrated)
- **FLANDERS,** Michel. Nasreddin the Wise. London. 1974. (Illustrated)
- **GARNIER,** Jean Paul. Nasreddin Hodscha. Munchen, 1965. (Illustrated)
- **GARNIER,** Jean Paul. Nasreddin Hodja et ses histoires Turques. Rene Julliard, Paris, 1958.
- **GEMİCİ,** Rasim. Contes de Nasreddin Hodja. Doğuş Ltd. Şti. Matbaası, Ankara, 1958. (Illustrated) (Second Edition 1960)
- **GEMİCİ,** Rasim. Nasreddin Hodja Stories. Doğuş Ltd. Ortaklığı Matbaası, Ankara, 1957. (Illustrated)
- **GEMİCİ,** Rasim. The Hodja for Children. Doğuş Ltd. Şti. Matbaası, Ankara, 1960. (Illustrated)
- **GIGLIESI,** Primerose and **FRIEND,** Robert C. . The Effendi and the Pregnant Pot-Uygur Folktales from China. New World Press, Beijing,

1982. (Illustrated)
- **GORDILEVSKIY,** V.A.. Anekdoti o Hoca Nasr-Ed-Dine. Porevod s turetskogo, stat'ya i kommentarii. Academia, Leningrad, 1936.
- **GORDLEVSKOGO,** V.A.. Anekdoti o Hodja Nasreddine. Akademiya Nauk SSR Institut Vostokovedeniya, Moskova, 1957. (Illustrated)
- **GÖÇMEN,** Olcay. Nasreddin Hoca. Doyuran Ofset, İstanbul, 1981. (Illustrated)
- **GÖKŞEN,** Enver Naci. Hoca'dan Fıkralar. (Stories From the Hodja). İyigün Yayınları, İstanbul, 1964. (Other Editions. 1966, 1971, 1973, 1977)
- **GÖLPINARLI,** Abdülbaki. Nasreddin Hoca. Remzi Kitabevi, İstanbul, 1961. (Illustrated)
- **GÜNEY,** Eflatun Cem. Nasreddin Hoca Fıkraları. (Tales of Nasreddin Hodja). Yeditepe Yayınları, İstanbul, 1957. (Illustrated)
- **GÜNEY,** Eflatun Cem. Nasreddin Hoca Fıkraları. (Tales of Nasreddin Hodja). Varlık Yayınları, İstanbul, 1962. (Illustrated) (Other Editions 1968, 1974)
- **GÜR,** A. Refik. Nasreddin Hoca, Hayatı Fıkraları Üzerine Fikri, Felsefi Bir İnceleme. (Nasreddin Hodja, An Intellectual and Philosophical Study on His Life and Stories). (Second Edition) Çeltüt Matbaası, İstanbul, 1959.
- **GÜRDİL,** Ömer. Resimli Nasreddin Hoca Fıkraları. (Illustrated Tales of Nasreddin Hodja). Şenyıldız Yayınevi, İstanbul, 1985.
- **GÜRGEN,** Fevzi. Resimli Nasreddin Hoca Fıkraları. (Illustrated Tales of Nasreddin Hodja). Sağlam Kitabevi, İstanbul, 1977.
- **İSAKOVİC,** Aliya. Nasruddin Hoca. Svetlost Yayınevi, Saroyova, 1985.
- **(İZBUDAK),** Veled Çelebi. Letaif-i Hoca Nasreddin. İkbal Kiitüphanesi, İstanbul, 1923.
- **KANIK,** Orhan Veli. Nasreddin Hoca, 70 Manzum Hikaye. (Nasreddin Hodja, 70 Stories In Verse). Narodna Prosveta, Sofya, 1968.
- **KANIK,** Orhan Veli. Nasreddin Hoca. Nave Makedoniya Yayınevi, Üsküp, 1964.
- **KANIK,** Orhan Veli. Nasreddin Hoca Hikayeleri, 70 Manzum Hikaye. (Tales of Nasreddin Hodja, 70 Tales In Verse). Doğan Kardeş Yayınları, İstanbul, 1949. (Other Editions 1953, 1954, 1957, 1970)
- **KAPLAN,** Mevlüt. Nasreddin Hoca. Özgür Eğitim Yayınları, İzmir. (Illustrated).
- **KARAHASAN,** Mustafa. Nasreddin Hodza i Njegov Humor. Knjizevna Novine, Belgrad, 1959.
- **KARAHASAN,** Mustafa. Nasreddin Hoca'nın Hikayeleri. (Stories of Nasreddin Hodja). Skopje, 1985.
- **KELSEY,** Alice Geer. Once the Hodja. Longmans-Green and Co., New York, Toronto, 1952 (Illustrated). (Other Editions 1954, 1957, 1958, 1959)
- **KOCAGÖZ,** Samim. Nasreddin Hoca Fıkraları. (Tales of Nasreddin Nadia). Yeditepe Yayınları, İstanbul 1972.
- **KOCATÜRK,** Vasfi Mahir. Nasreddin Hoca. İstanbul, 1954. (Illustrated).
- **KORGUNAL,** Muharrem Zeki. Nasreddin Hoca ve Fıkraları. (Nasreddin Hodja and His Stories). Yusuf Ziya Kitabevi, İstanbul, 1937.
- **KORGUNAL,** Muharrem Zeki. Nasreddin Hoca ve Fıkraları. (Nasreddin Hodja and His Stories). Emniyet Kitabevi, İstanbul, 1941. (Illustrated).
- **KORGUNAL,** Muharrem Zeki. Nasreddin Hoca ve Fıkraları. (Nasreddin Hodja and His Jokes). Emniyet Kitabevi, İstanbul, 1973.
- **KORGUNAL,** Muharrem Zeki. Tam ve Resimli Nasreddin Hoca Fıkraları. (Illustrated)
Tales of Nasreddin Hodja). Ak-Un Basımevi, İstanbul, 1944. (Second Edition 1947)
- **KOZ,** M. Sabri. Nasreddin Hoca'dan Fıkralar. (Stories From Nasreddin Hodja). Serhat Yayınları, İstanbul, 1984. (Illustrated).
- **KÖKLÜGİLLER,** Ahmet. Nasreddin Hoca. Koza Yayınları, İstanbul, 1978.
- **KÖPRÜLÜ,** M. Fuad. Manzum Nasreddin Hoca Fıkraları. (Tales of Nasreddin Hodja In Verse). Üçdal Neşriyat, İstanbul, 1980.
- **KÖPRÜLÜZADE,** Mehmet Fuad. Nasreddin Hoca. Kanaat Kütüphanesi ve Matbaası, İstanbul, 1919.
- **KÖSLÜ,** M. Emin. Resimli Nasreddin Hoca Latifeleri. (Illustrated Tales of Nasreddin Hodja). Yusuf Ziya Kitabevi, İstanbul, 1936.
- **KUNOS,** Dr. Ignacz. Anecdotes of Nasr-Eddin. Budapest, 1899.
- **KUNOS,** Dr. Ignacz. A Törük Hodzsa Trefai. Budapest.
- **KUNOS,** Dr. Ignacz. A Törük Hodzsa Trefai. Nasreddin mesternek a közel és tavol keleten ismert bölcs és hires kisazsiai hodzsanak csalafinsagai es mulatsagos esetei. Gyoma, 1926.
- **KURGAN,** Şükrü. Anekdota tou Nasrettin Khotza. Apodosis ek tou tovrkikou prototipou Akhilleos S. Bapheide. M. Pekhlibanides kai Sia A.E., Athens, 1961. (Illustrated).
- **KURTULUŞ,** Nevzat. Nasreddin Hoca Fıkraları. (Tales of Nasreddin Hodja). Nevzat Yayınevi, Ankara, 1978. (Illustrated).
- **Lİ-KEH-NAN.** Turk Mizahı Nasreddin Hoca. (Turkish Humorist Nasreddin Hodja). Taiwan, 1980, (Chinese)
- **MAHEN,** Jiri. Janosik ulicka odvahy Nasreddin. Statni Nakladatel stvi Krasne Literatury a Umenei, Praha, 1962.
- **MALLOUF,** H.. Plaisanteries de Nasr-Eddin Khodja. İzmir, 1854.
- **MALLOUF,** H.. Plaisanteries de Khodja Nasr-ed-Din Efendi, İstanbul, 1859.
- **MANAVOĞLU,** İhsan. Resimlerle Büyük Nasreddin Hoca. Ak Kitabevi, İstanbul, 1957. (Illustrated).
- **MANDIL,** David. Resimlerle Nasreddin Hoca Albümü. Resimler: Ponti. (Illustrated Album of Nasreddin Hodja. Illustr. by Ponti). Hüsnütabiat Matbaası, İstanbul, 1977.
- **MARDRUS,** J.C.. Le Livre des Mille nuits et une Nuit. Paris, 1904.
- **MASAO,** Mori. Nasreddin Hoca Konagatari. Tokyo, 1961.
- **MEFHARET,** Nazmi. Nasreddin Hoca Hikayeleri. (Stories of Nasreddin Hodja). Hilmi Kitabevi, İstanbul, 1928.
- **MILLE,** Pierre. Nasreddin et son epouse. Calmann-Levy, Paris, 1910.
- **MOLLA,** Nasreddin Latifeleri. İzdatel stvo Akademii Nauk Azerbaydjanskoy SSR. Baku, 1966. (Illustrated).
- **MÖRER,** Alfred. Contes Choisis de Nasreddin Hodja. Galeri Minyatür Yayınları, İstanbul, 1975. (Illustrated).
- **MÖRER,** Alfred. 200 Contes Choisis de Nasreddin Hodja. Baha Matbaası, İstanbul, 1969. (Illustrated).
- **MÖRER,** Alfred. 202 Jokes of Nasreddin Hodja. Galeri Minyatür Yayınları, İstanbul, (Illustrated).
- **MÖRER,** Alfred. 202 Witze von Nasreddin Hodja. Galeri Minyatür Yayınları, İstanbul. (Illustrated).
- **MURAT,** Hikmet. One Day the Hodja. Tarhan Publications, Ankara, 1959. (Illustrated).
- **MÜLLENDORF,** Dr. E.. Nasreddin-Hodja. Ein Osmanischer Eulenspiegel. Oldenburg, 1891.
- **NAMETAU,** Alija. 101 Stajeden Nasrudin Hodzina Sala. Sarajevo, 1960.
- **NASREDDİN,** Hoca. Derya Yayınları, İstanbul, 1959. (Illustrated).

- **NASREDDİN** Hoca. Illustr. by Mim Uykusuz, foreword by Aziz Nesin. Selek Yayınevi, İstanbul, 1959.
- **NASREDDİN** Hoca. Serhat Yayınları, İstanbul, 1982.
- **NASREDDİN** Hodscha. Geschichten Buntbebilderts. And Yayınları Koll. Şti., İstanbul, 1977. (Illustrated).
- **NASREDDİN** Hodza: Njegove sale, dostke i lakidje u pripodjothama od Mehemmeda Teffika, Prevod's. Nemackog. U. Nuvom, Sedu, 1903.
- **NASREDDİN** Hoca'dan Seçmeler. Burcu Yayınevi, İstanbul, 1983.
- **NASREDDİN** Hoca Fıkraları. Foreword by Ismail Hakkı Danişmend. Tasvir Neşriyatı, İstanbul, 1944. (Illustrated).
- **NASREDDİN** Hoca Hikayeleri. Maarif Kütüphanesi, İstanbul, 1947. (Illustrated). (Other Editions 1956, 1958, 1959, 1964)
- **NASREDDİN** Hocayi Gyanki. Manguiyunn Tbrotzafani srçam, İstanbul, 1955.
- **NASRODIN** Hoca, nyegove sole dosetke i lokırdiye u'pripovtètkamo. Belgrad, 1923.
- **NASRUDDİN** Efendija, njegove sale, dosjetke i njegova filozofija. Sarajevo.
- **NASRUDİN** Hodza, "knjigo puno sale i smijeha". Mostor, 1930.
- **NEVADİRİ** Nasreddin-ir-Rûmiyy-il meşhur bi Cüha. Kahire, 1862. (Second Edition 1883).
- **OKUR,** Özlem. Nasreddin Hoca'dan Seçme Fıkralar. Nil Yayınevi, İstanbul, 1982.
- **ORBAY,** Kemaleddin Chukru. Vie de Nasreddin Hodja. Editions de la Librairie Kanaat, İstanbul. (Illustrated).
- **ÖNDER,** Mehmet. Güldüren Gerçek: Nasreddin Hoca'nın Hayat Hikayesi. (The Life Story of Nasreddin Hodja). Nasreddin Hoca Yayınları, Akşehir, 1964.
- **ÖNDER,** Mehmet. Nasreddin Hoca. İş Bankası Kültür Yayınları, İstanbul, 1971.
- **ÖZBEK,** Niyazi. Nasreddin Hoca. Ak-Ün Basımevi, İstanbul, 1946. (Illustrated).
- **ÖZER,** Kemal. Nasreddin Hoca. Cem Yayınevi, İstanbul, 1973. (Illustrated). (Other Editions 1976, 1980)
- **ÖZGÜR,** Günseli. Hodja's Retort. Ho1p Shuppan Publishore, Japan, 1984.
- **ÖZGÜR,** Günseli. Nasreddin Hoca. Remzi Kitabevi, İstanbul, 1984. (Illustrated)
- **ÖZGÜREL,** Mehmet. Nasreddin Hoca'dan Seçme Fıkralar. (Selected Tales of Nasreddin Nadia). Zühal Yayınları, İstanbul, 1970. (Illustrated).
- **PANN,** Anton. Nasratin Hogea. Inteleptul Arghir şi Nepotul san Anadam. Bucureşti, 1908.
- **PANN,** Anton. Nazdravaniile Iui Nasratin Hogea. Culese şi versifivcate de Anton Pann. Bucureşti, 1853.
- **PARNWELL,** E.C.. Tales of the Hodja. London, 1969. (Illustrated).
- **PIO,** V.. Lustiger historier om Nasreddin Hodja. Copenhagen, 1902.
- **POSURICE** i sale Nasredina. Tisak i naklada kniizare Lav Hartmann, Zagreb.
- **RAMAZANİ,** Muhammed. Molla Nasreddin. Haver Matbaası, Tahran, 1940.
- **REHM,** Hermann Siegfried. Nasreddin, der Schelm, Fahrten, Meinungen and Taten des lachenden Philosophen Nasreddin Hodsche, des Türkischen Eulenpiegel. Schuster Loeffler, Berlin-Leipzig, 1916.
- **RESİMLİ** Nasreddin Hoca Fıkraları. (Illustrated Tales of Nasreddin Hodja). Bolayır Yayınları, İstanbul., 1967. (Other Editions 1970, 1972).
- **SAD,** Novi. Nasreddin Hoca. Belgrad, 1903.
- **SANDAŞ,** Sayit. Nasreddin Hoca. Serhat Yayınları, İstanbul, 1984.
- **SARAÇOĞLU,** Nasreddin Hoca. Eskişehir Sanatçıları Birliği Derneği Yayınları, Eskişehir, 1979.
- **SARIYÜCE,** Hasan Latif. Manzum Nasreddin Hoca Hikayeleri. (Tales of Nasreddin Hoca In Verse). Güneş Yayınları, Ankara, 1978.
- **SCHWANKE** des Hodscha, Nasreddin. Mit Holzatichen von Wilfried Blocher. Frankfurt, 1964.
- **SHAH,** İdries. The Exploits of the Incomparable Mulla Nasrudin. Buttler and Tanner Ltd., London, 1967.
- **SHAH,** İdries. The Pleasantries of Incredible Mulla Nasrudin. Jonathan Cape, London, 1968. (Illustrated).
- **SİVRİ,** Ismail. Nasreddin Hoca. Milliyet Yayınları Ltd. Şti., İstanbul 1977.
- **SOKO,** Ziya Şakir. Nasreddin Hoca. Maarif Kitaphanesi, İstanbul, 1940. (Illustrated). (Other Editions 1943, 1944, 1956)
- **SOKO,** Ziya Şakir. Nasreddin Hoca'nın Hayatı ve Hikayeleri. (Nasreddin Hodja, His Life and His Stories). Tan Evi Matbaası, İstanbul, 1934. (Illustrated). (Second Edition 1939)
- **SOLOVEV,** Leonid. Povest o Hodja Nasreddine. Moskova, 1957. (Second Edition 1958)
- **SÖNMEZ,** Tekin. Bizim Hoca Nasreddin. Yansıma Yayınları, İstanbul, 1981. (Illustrated).
- **SPIES,** Dr. Otto. Hodscha Nasreddin. Ein Türkischer Eulenspiegel. Veltgeist-Bucher, Verlags-Gesellschaft, Berlin, 1928.
- **SREMATS,** Stevan. Nasradin-Hoca, nyegove dosetke i budologsine u pricama. Belgrad, 1894.
- **ŞAINEAU,** Lazar. Nasradin Hogea. Revisto Nuva, Bucureşti, 1890.
- **ŞENER,** Dr. Nuran. Nasreddin Hoca. Milliyet Gazetesi ve KAOB İşbirliği Yayını, İstanbul, 1967
- **ŞENYILDIZ,** Aykut. Seçilmiş Nasreddin Hoca Latifeleri. (Selected Jokes of Nasreddin Hodja). Şenyıldız Yayınevi, İstanbul, 1974. (Illustrated). (Second Edition 1981).
- **ŞOP,** İvan. Nasreddinove Metamorfoze. Institut za Knyijevnost i Umetnost, Belgrad, 1973.
- **TATLIK,** Erişiddin. Nasreddin Efendi. Urunçi, 1979.
- **TEHMASIB,** M.T.. Molla Nasreddin Latifeleri. Azarbeycan SSR Elmler Akademiyası Neşriyatı, Baku, 1956. (Illustrated). (Other Editions 1958, 1965)
- **TEKMAN,** Mehmet Şinasi. Nasreddin Hoca Şiirleri. (Nasreddin Hodja Poems). Lelkoşe, 1954.
- **TOKMAKÇIOĞLU,** Erdoğan. Nasreddin Hoca. Sinan Yayınları, İstanbul, 1971.
- **TOKMAKÇIOĞLU,** Erdoğan. Bütün Yönleriyle Nasreddin Hoca. Kültür Bakanlığı Yayınları, Ankara, 1981.
- **TOMOV,** I.K.. Nasreddin Hodja i Hitr Petr. Svistov, 1896.
- **TOPÇUOĞLU,** Ümit Sinan. Nasreddin Hoca Rahmetulah-i Aleyh ve Latifeleri. Üst Yayınları, İstanbul, 1980.
- **TUNCER,** Ferit Ragıp. Renkli Resimlerle Nasreddin Hoca. (Nasreddin Hodja with Colored Pictures). Inkilap ve Aka Kitabevi, İstanbul, 1984.
- **TUTKUN,** Kâmile. Nasreddin Hoca Fıkraları. Taner Yayınevi, İstanbul, 1983. (Second Edition 1984)
- **ÜLKÜTAŞIR,** Mehmet Şakir - **ÖZTELLİ,** Cahit. Nasreddin Hoca. Turk Etnografya ve Folklor Derneği Yayınları, Ankara 1964.
- **ÜNLÜ,** Necdet. Hoca'dan Fıkralar. (Tales From the Hodja). Ülkü Yayınevi, İstanbul, 1981.

- **VALAVANI,** Joakeim. Ho Nasreddin Chotzas Byzanttinon. Atina, 1888.
- **VULCHEV,** Velichko. Artful Peter and Nasreddin Hodja. From the History of the Bulgarian Folk Anecdote. Bulgarian Academy of Sciences Publications, Sofya, 1975.
- **WALKER,** Barbara K.. Watermelons, Walnuts and the Wisdom of Allah and Other Tales of the Hoca. Parent Magazine Press, New York, 1967.
- **WERNER,** Granz von. Nasreddin Chodja. Ein Osmanischer Eulenspiegel von Murad Efendi. Oldenburg, 1878.
- **YAGAN,** Turgay. Stories of Hodja. Öney Matbaası, İstanbul, 1972. (Illustrated).
- **YAŞAROĞLU,** Ahmet Halit. Nasreddin Hoca Fıkraları Ahmet Halit Kitabevi, İstanbul, 1950. (Illustrated).
- **YAŞAROĞLU,** Ahmet Halit. Nasrydun Hoca priçei dosetke. Sarajevo, 1953.
- **YILMAZKAYA,** Mustafa. Nasreddin Hoca'dan Seçmeler. Günaydın Kitabevi, İstanbul, 1972. (Illustrated).
- **YİĞİTLER,** H. Zekai. Nasreddin Hoca. Esin Yayınları, İstanbul, 1983. (Illustrated).
- **YORGANCI,** Orhan. Şiir Diliyle Nasreddin Hoca Fıkraları. (Tales of Nasreddin Hodja In Verse). Barış Matbaası, Tokat, 1977. (Illustrated).
- **YURDATAP,** Selami Münir. Büyük Nasreddin Hoca Fıkraları. (Great Nasreddin Hodja Tales). Bozkurt Matbaası, İstanbul, 1975.
- **YURDATAP,** Selami Münir. Resimli Tam Nasreddin Hoca Fıkraları. (Illustrated Tales of Nasreddin Hodja). Çınar Matbaası, İstanbul, 1966.
- **YUSUF,** Nevzat - **YUSUF,** Nermin. Nasreddin Hoga'ga dair Masallar. Kriterion Kitap Üyü, Bucureşti, 1983.
- **ZAPARTA,** (Ertuğrul Şevket Pişkin). Nasreddin Latifeleri Külliyatı. Ankara, 1943.
- **ZEYNALLI,** H.. Molla Nasreddin Mezhekeleri. Baku, 1927.
- **ZIMMANICHI,** N.. Vyber tekstov Tureckion opo vidania Choday Nasraddina. Varşova, 1951.
- **ZNAMENJITYYJO,** Tatarskiye suty Achmet Achai - Nasreddin Odeaj. Odessa, 1904.

BIOGRAPHICAL NOTES

Aziz Nesin was born in 1915 in Istanbul. He studied at the War College, and Applied Sciences Vocational School. Later he attended The Fine Arts Academy in Istanbul for two years.
He entered the world of literature through his poetry, first publishing under the pen name Vedia Nesin. He worked as a journalist for several newspapers, ran a grocery store and a bookstore, and acted as a bookkeeper and photographer. With the famous Turkish writer Sabahattin Ali he published the satirical magazines Markopagt, Malumpagi, and Merhumpaşa.
He spent the years 1947 to 1950 in jail because of his political articles and translations.
In 1955 he began concentrating on satirical stories and essays; started the publishing house DiiOn and the satirical magazine Ziibiik. By this time he was recognized as a new and strong writer, preferring the local language of the Anatolian people rather than the stilted flowery language of Ottoman literature. Aziz Nesin is industrious and prolific: writing seems to come easy to him. An acute observer of the ironies in life he cleverly incorporates these observations into humorous stories.
He is the winner of many international awards. Over one hundred of his works have been published, many of which have been translated into other languages. He is also well known as a playwright.
With the income from his works Nesin has etsablished a foundation to care for orphans and poor children. He continues to work with the foundation and to be active in collective and individual work dedicated to social development, democracy and fundemental rights and freedoms for all people.
Having recently suffered two heart attacks, Nesin was asked by a friend, "Where have you been?" He answered, "I'm running from Gabriel."
Talat S. Halman was Turkey's first Minister of Culture and later served as his country's first Ambassador for Cultural Affairs. Currently he is a Professor of Near Eastern Languages and Literatures at New York University. Formerly he was at Columbia University, the University of Pennsylvania, and Princeton University for many years. His books include Contemporary Turkish Literature, Yunus Emre and His Mystical Poetry, Modern Turkish Literature, Yunus Emre and Magnificent Poet, Shadows of Love and A Last Lullaby (both containing his original poems in English), Living Poets of Turkey, Turkish Legends and Folk Poems, and many other books. Among his books in Turkish are four collections of his poems, the Sonnets of Shakespeare, a massive volume of the poetry of ancient civilizations, and others. In 1971, he was decorated Knight Grand Cross (G.B.E.) by Queen Elizabeth II. In 1986 Columbia University awarded him the Thornton Wilder Prize for Translation. He is co-author (with Metin And) of the Dost book entitled Mevlana Celaleddin Rumi and the Whirling Dervishes. Some of his books have been translated into French, Hebrew, Persian, Urdu, and Hindu.
Since 1991 he is a Member of the Executive Board of UNESCO.
Zeki Findikoşlu was born in 1946 in Iznik, Turkey. He spent his childhood in small villages, and towns in Anatolia.
Findikoşlu graduated from The Fine Arts Academy of Istanbul with a Masters Degree in Fine Arts, specializing in painting. In 1973 he moved to the U.S.A. and continued his education at the Corcoran School of Arts; then earned a M.F.A. degree in Visual Communication Design from The George Washington University.
He has been a professor of Fine Arts at the University of the District of Columbia and Trinity College, and also has worked as a freelance artist for many organizations. His art work has included the catalogue of National Gallery of Art's "The Age of Süleyman the Magnificent Exhibition".
His art work takes its subjects from Turkish culture and folklore. His original prints have been exhibited in over 30 one man shows in the U.S.A. and Turkey. His works have received many awards and been exhibited in more than 20 juried shows.
In 1987-1988 Findikoşlu was on Sabbatical leave in Turkey. During this period he produced the Nasrettin Hoca illustrations, and conducted research on traditional Turkish designs, and their application to contemporary art.
Findtkoşlu continues to work out of his studio in Washington D.C.. He is represented by the Franz Baader Gallery in Washington D.C., and Gallery Baraz in Istanbul.

Art Selection and Design:

Focus Basım


Illustrations:

Evrim İKİZ


Translation:

Talat HALMAN


Colour Separation and Films:

Doğa Basım


Printing:

Doğa Basım

ISBN 978-975-7499-46-6


SILK ROAD TOURISTIC PUBLICATIONS

DOST YAYINLARI LTD. ŞTİ.

Galip Dede Caddesi No: 85/A Beyoğlu, İstanbul -TÜRKİYE

Tel: 0212-245 31 41   Fax: 0212-245 75 83